The Fundamentals of Email Marketing

7 Things You Need to Know
to Achieve Success

Written by Zach Heller

ISBN: 1463627238
ISBN-13: 978-1463627232

To my parents, who always had a way of instilling confidence in me, and without whom nothing would be possible.

ABOUT THE AUTHOR

Zach Heller is owner and operator of Zach Heller Marketing. His blog, *"I" of the Consumer*, serves to provide commentary and tips on marketing in the digital age.

Zach is a marketing professional with experience in branding, digital marketing, direct response, and marketing communications. He currently serves as the Director of Marketing for Distance Education Co. LLC, a medium-sized education and publishing company which operates two schools in Manhattan.

Zach has a bachelor's degree in Marketing and Economics from the University of Delaware.

For more from Zach Heller, visit www.zachhellermarketing.com.

Table of Contents

INTRODUCTION

"42% of consumers said the best way to receive ads for sales and specials is via email." - *Econsultancy* "How We Shop in 2010: Habits and Motivations of Consumers" (2010)

Based on the statistic above, it is clear that if you are not using email as a regular part of your marketing in 2011, you are missing out on a large group of consumers. Not only that, but you are missing out on one of the most effective ways to communicate with customers and potential customers in an age dominated by the internet.

Selling is not what it used to be, and marketing is changing faster than the world around us. The way to get your message in front of consumers is constantly evolving. And email is still a growing part of that mix.

This book is meant to show you, in seven different ways, how and why you should be using email as a marketing tool. In the sections that follow, I will outline the different aspects of email marketing. I will provide the statistics and proof that will show you the right way to do things, and the wrong.

These fundamentals are based on years of testing to discover proven methods of email marketing and how it can tie into a larger online marketing strategy. By no means will this book be the be all and end all. If I told you that, you'd have to question my sanity. Email, just like all other aspects of online marketing, is an ever-changing beast: what works today may not work six months from now. In this book, I will give you the fundamentals so you can start trying new things, and asking the right questions of your marketing campaigns.

The first section, WHAT, focuses on exactly what you want to send. This may seem like a simple question to answer, but there is a lot more that goes into constructing a marketing email than you might think.

The second section, WHY, focuses on strategy. Defining a purpose for each email is important, so you want to set goals and have something on which to base your measurement of success.

The third section, HOW, is all about answering the question: how do you get your contacts? In order to start an email marketing campaign, you have to have email addresses in the "contacts" field.

Next, we discuss WHEN. This section covers everything you need to know about the best time to send out your emails.

Once you know when to email, you need to know WHERE to email. In this section we will discuss the many options available to you in helping to create and send your marketing emails.

The sixth section, WHO, focuses on your contacts. Knowing who they are and what they want, is an important part of communicating with them. It can change the messages you send, the frequency at which you send them, and the best time to reach them.

The final section discusses the importance of continual testing and tracking in order to improve your email marketing campaigns. I've said it before and I'll say it again: email marketing – and all other forms of online marketing – is an ever- changing beast. It takes time and energy to make it work, and testing new things will help you stay one step ahead of the other marketers out there competing for the consumers' attention.

Let the games begin!

SECTION ONE: WHAT

Let's assume you're reading this because you've decided that email marketing is a good idea. Whether you're a business owner who's interested in using email as part of your marketing efforts to grow your business, a marketer who thinks that you could help your company by introducing or improving your email marketing campaigns, or just someone looking to learn more about the art of email marketing for your own benefit, the next step is easy. What do you send?

This section will focus on what goes into constructing an email, and all of the things that you have to keep in mind when creating your campaign.

The first thing to think about is the subject line. The subject line is usually the first thing that people see when looking at their emails and can determine immediately whether your email gets opened or deleted.

In marketing, there are small battles that you have to win in order to win the war. Consumers are constantly making choices, little ones that can affect you in big ways. Opening the email is a big battle. If they don't open it, they can't read it. And if they don't read it, they won't click through or buy anything from it. The subject line is all about winning that first battle.

> "Emails with shorter subject lines significantly outperformed emails with longer subject lines." - *MailerMailer* (2008)

A good subject line is short and to the point. The shorter the subject, the better – as long as you can get a message across. Since most email providers have limited space to display a subject, a long subject line is often cut off and thus loses its meaning. Keep it short, and keep the most important part of the subject at the beginning; this will give it the best chance of being seen.

60 characters is a good rule of thumb for subject line length. Anything longer may get cut off, or may be too long to grab anyone's attention.

Best Subject Line Ever

instead of...

This is the best subject line you have ever read

The second thing to note about subject lines is that personalization *used* to be very popular. Today, when people see their name in the subject line of an email, they know it's a marketing message. It's an easy way to get under someone's skin because it just looks "scammy." Avoid it.

Third, give them a reason to open your message. Is there a special offer that they are interested in? Then put it in the subject line. You don't necessarily have to spell it out for them, but let them know that by opening the email, they'll be privy to something special. This serves as a call to action and gives them a reason to do what you want them to do.

But in doing this, avoid the word "free" and dollar signs ($) as often as possible. Many email providers will mark an email as spam if they see those in the subject line. You want to avoid that at all cost. Getting into the inbox is another one of those small battles, one which we will discuss in more detail later.

Special Discount Offer from "I" of the Consumer

instead of...

Joe, a Free Gift for you inside

Now that you've gotten the basics of a subject line down, let's move on to the next most important part of an email: the From Address. The From Address is the email address and contact name of the sender which in this case, is you. The way you represent yourself or your company in the From Address matters and can affect the decision of a consumer to open the email.

Depending on what email client a person uses, the From Address and the subject line are the two things that show up before you open up an email to read it. On some clients, the From Address is even more important than the subject line because it shows up first.

It's important that you be as clear as possible when it comes to the From Address. Clearly identify the company or the specific email list that the recipient signed up for, because that will help put them at ease. If a person receives an email from someone that they don't recognize, they are ten times more likely to hit the "delete" button (or worse, the "mark as spam" button).

Use the most recognizable brand or list name, e.g. Whole Foods or Netflix Offers, as the From name. There is no reason to get creative here. In fact, this is one case where being creative will hurt you.

As for the email address, it's best to use something like generic@yourmainwebsite.com (info@zachhellermarketing.com or offers@papajohns.com). Again, this helps the customer or potential customer recognize where the email is coming from, and reminds them why they're interested.

Now you've gotten the Subject Line and From Address taken care of, it's time to move into the main body of the email. Within the body there are a number of factors which may change depending on the nature of the email, such as the copy, any images, and your hyperlinks.

Let's start with the copy.

You will hear over and over again, in reference to many different things, that content is king. And any good email campaign includes good copy. But good copy can take on multiple meanings.

If the sole purpose of your email is to generate immediate sales, your copy should be short and sweet, giving the potential customer a reason to click through and purchase. If you're going for more of a Newsletter type email, then you want the copy to provide valuable information to your subscriber, something they cannot get anywhere else.

Your copy gives you a chance to stand out from the crowd. In the world of email marketing, you're fighting for space in the market. The average adult in the United States receives approximately seven commercial emails in a day, with many receiving more than that. The odds are against your email being read, so the copy needs to be intriguing enough to hold the attention of those people who do actually open the email and start to read. We will go into this in more detail later in the book.

Another important thing to remember as you write the copy is this: you should always write with the reader in mind. Make sure that the writing style is expected and easy to understand. While I do not recommend dumbing down your emails, it is important to keep in mind that something on a lower reading level is more likely to be read, understood, and shared by the masses.

*Try running your text through a readability scorer to measure how it stacks up: http://www.addedbytes.com/lab/readability-score/.

Make your copy relatable and be informal where appropriate. Tell your story to the reader quickly and easily, moving them along to a call to action ('purchase now', 'click here for more', 'download today'). In email, as in most marketing messages, saying more with fewer words makes it more likely your message will get across.

Another very important thing to remember when writing your copy is that many people will read your email on a phone. This is a point I will come back to in every section. The use of smartphones to access the web and read email is more popular today than ever before, and that trend will continue to grow. To get through to someone on a phone, emails need to be shorter and more poignant, because the easiest thing to do is click delete.

Within the copy, you will most likely want to include links. Links should be used to direct people where you want them to go. You want to be careful not to flood your emails with links, but to include enough links to the right places so that your message gets across. Some of your customers might skim the message and click on a link as soon as they see it. Others might prefer to read the entire email before clicking.

A good rule of thumb is to have at least one link at the top, for someone who won't read the email, and at least two more as you move down the body of the email. In numerous tests, more links meant more clicks. But like anything, there is a limit. At a certain point, if the majority of your email is a hyperlink, it makes it look like spam.

Another point to remember is that you want to give the customer very few paths to take, meaning your links should all point to where you want the reader to go. The more you send them down different paths, the less likely it is they will find their way back. Fewer options most often leads to more sales.

The final elements of an email worth talking about are the images. If you are sending out an HTML email, which most commercial emails are, then you'll most likely want to include some form of imagery. If you do it in the right way, this will help your email stand out from the crowd.

Some companies choose to use a webpage-like structure with a full border, banner on the top, and the footer on the bottom. Others choose to use images a little more sparingly, highlighting something about the offer or providing a photo that compliments a story. They both work.

The best way to use images is to 1) highlight any aspect of the offer that comes across in a picture better than it would in written word, and 2) familiarize the reader with a certain look or style.

Highlight the offer!

This means provide a picture of the product you're selling, a picture of someone using it and the benefit they're receiving, or maybe a bonus that you get if you act now. It does not mean stock photography or a logo. These are boring uses of images and should be left out for the purposes of marketing.

Familiarize!

Many companies make the look of an email similar to the look of the page readers end up on when they click through. This is a form of setting the mood, and making the reader – the potential customer – feel comfortable when they click through. The use of similar photos, colors, buttons, borders, and font makes the transition from email to sales process seamless and increases the likelihood of conversion.

Having said all of that, there are times you don't want to use any images.

Images do not immediately show up in most email clients, requiring an extra click from the reader to display them. At times, you could lose the impact of your message when someone skips over this step and views your email without any images. To save yourself from this lost opportunity, make sure that the point of the message comes across with or without images.

Also, the use of images and HTML in emails immediately signals to the reader that this is a marketing message. If you have a devoted fanbase that looks forward to receiving email from you, this won't hurt the effectiveness of your campaign. But some cases might call for an email that blends in, making it more likely that someone who would not normally read it, does. In these cases, using a plain text email might make more sense. It seems a little more personal and call for a greater number of people to read it.

We've reached the end of the first section, and hopefully you have a much better idea of what it takes to construct an email. It's more than just what you want to say; each element should be carefully crafted to serve a purpose. But what is that purpose? Section Two will help us answer that question.

SECTION TWO: WHY

"247 billion emails were sent each day in 2009. That's an email every 0.00000035 seconds." - *e-Dialog* "Manifesto for E-mail Marketers: Consumers Demand Relevance" (2010)

Most marketers and companies today know that they should be incorporating email into their marketing mix. But there is no point in having email just to say that you use it. There is a purpose to email marketing, and that purpose may vary from company to company.

If you are going to start a new email marketing campaign, or even if you already have one that you are looking to improve, it's important to start with a goal and build from there.

Now I can't begin to pretend to understand your company or your goals as well as you can, but I can make an educated guess about what you're doing and what kind of message you'd like to send. There are a few basic types of marketing emails which I will use to demonstrate the importance of setting expectations and then measuring success against those expectations.

There are four basic categories of marketing emails that we will use to form our discussion:

1. Newsletter
2. Auto-Response
3. Standard Offer Announcement
4. Deadline or Deal Email

The first type of marketing email is what we will refer to as a Newsletter. A Newsletter is any regular email that goes out to a list of people who asked for it. It contains news, updates, etc. but does not contain a direct sales message.

A large majority of people in the United States subscribe to at least one Newsletter. Newsletters are a popular form of email marketing as they are the least intrusive and the least "pushy." The main purpose of a Newsletter, from the business perspective, is to create brand loyalty. By putting your brand in front of interested people more often, you are building the brand and creating some devotion on the part of the consumer base.

Your Newsletter should contain unique content, content that is not widely available outside of the Newsletter, or that is assembled in an easy-to-view way for the reader. The more it applies to your core business, the better, because it gives you a chance to strengthen the brand in a positive way.

Some examples of how a Newsletter can work for various businesses are: an accounting firm using a monthly Newsletter to share tax tips and personal finance advice; a local brewery using a weekly Newsletter to alert subscribers of new beer creations and tastings; a non-profit group using a quarterly Newsletter to share stories of inspiration and progress with their subscribers and members.

In a Newsletter, content is most important because good content will be shared with others. Subscribers may forward an email or share a story with non-subscribers, increasing the impact of each email and bringing in new customers or brand followers.

Avoid "selling" to your Newsletter list. They signed up for a reason, and you should not stray from the message from Newsletter to Newsletter.

The second type of marketing email is what we'll refer to as the Auto-Response. An Auto-Response is a prepared email (or series of emails) that goes out to a person after they perform some specified action.

For example, if I am interested in attending a school to improve my photography skills, I might fill out a form and request a course catalog. That school, having now collected my email address, will most likely send me an email about how great their course is. That email is standard, going out automatically to anyone who fills out that form.

A standard Auto-Response email allows you to follow up (or confirm) something with the consumer, without any real man hours. Once the email is complete and the system for sending it is set up, it's a hands-off marketing tool that is worth its weight in gold.

Companies use Auto-Response emails to confirm when someone has signed up for an event, to follow up with attendees of a meeting or webinar, or to provide more information on a product or service that a potential customer has shown interest in.

Some Auto-Response emails are used to sell, others are used to share information. Both work from a marketing perspective, inspiring confidence in a company's ability to keep customers informed with regular email contact – even though it's all automated.

The third type of marketing email is one that I call the Standard Offer Announcement. The Standard Offer Announcement is any discount or special, announced via email, which is not part of an Auto-Response series.

Companies will use these types of emails to reach out to their existing customers, former customers, or non-customers with a special offer. These can be emails that go out to your own list, or to a list you buy the rights to use. They are usually one-time emails announcing or reminding people of a deal or event.

The email is meant to create response, usually in the form of sales or signups, from readers. In that respect, emails in this category are getting close to what many consumers view as spam. They are the more traditional form of email marketing, used to generate sales from consumers who may or may not be interested in what you have to offer.

When sending these types of emails, it's important to be clear why you are sending this offer. Tell the reader right away why they're getting the message and how they can avoid receiving more. This prevents complaints you might get over the phone or via email, and will prevent your readers from marking the email as spam, a hugely negative event which can affect your ability to send future emails. (We will discuss this in more depth in Sections Three and Five.)

The important aspects of these emails are headlines and calls to action. Those people that are interested in the offer should be able to quickly learn about it, and know what the next step is. Direct them to a simple sign-up or checkout process. These types of emails will have lower open and click-through rates than either Newsletters or Auto-Response emails most times, but good ones will make you money.

The fourth type of marketing email we will discuss is the Deadline or Deal Email. Groupon has made this type of email famous. The best example of a Deadline Email is any email that screams "Limited Time" or "Today Only." Companies use emails like this to generate a large amount of interest (usually in the form of sales) in a special discount or upcoming event.

They are the riskiest form of email marketing but, done right, can also be the most lucrative. The goal of these emails is not to create long-term brand loyalty or interest. It is strictly to sell, and sell now.

I say that this is the riskiest type of email, because it is the most likely to come across as spam. But if a reader is expecting it, and the offer is good enough to get their attention, it can have major payouts. Groupon tells people specifically that they will receive an email every day with a new deal in their neighborhood, and they deliver on that.

To make this type of email work for you, it's important that those people receiving the emails are interested. Certainly, you can't reach all of them, but the deal should be big enough that it begs for attention. If today is the last day to get 20% off anything in the store, and I am on the regular mailing list for your store, I might want to know about it.

These messages should be short and sweet with a direct announcement of the deal in the subject line. Don't try to trick anyone here. Again, an easy and loud call to action is important to get those interested readers on the right path.

Using a combination of two, three, or four of the email types above will make sense for most companies. Newsletters stand out as a no-brainer, as long as you have the capacity to keep up with one and get it out on time. They are easy to get started, and you can use incentives to generate interest and get subscribers. Deal emails and Standard Offer Announcements will do the most to increase sales, but need to be dealt with more carefully than a Newsletter. Refer back to Section One when constructing these emails.

The email strategy for your company will comprise one or more of the types of emails above. The purpose of those emails may vary each time they are generated or sent, but just like your brand, the overall look and feel should be consistent. They are all forms of communication with consumers in the digital world, and a consistent message will go a long way toward strengthening your brand and getting attention.

In Section Three, we will discuss another important part of that email strategy, how you get the names and email addresses that you plan to send to.

SECTION THREE: HOW

How are you getting the email addresses that you are going to send to? Where are you collecting them? Why are people giving them to you? What do they expect?

So many questions to ask, but they're all important ones. One of the most overlooked aspects of email marketing is the collection of names.

There are a few ways to collect names, and each will give you a different result when you start to email them.

1. **You can purchase lists.**

You can buy names from a database based on a number of criteria. These are the names of people collected by other companies in some manner. They've never received an email from you, assumedly, and they are not very receptive to your emails. You will have to work very hard and make your offer absolutely magnificent to get their attention.

Within this category you can email those names yourself, or you can prepare an email that the owner of the list will send out. The second option is preferable, believe me. Even though you lose some control of the process, you are protecting your reputation as an email sender (something we'll talk more about in Section Five) and you're making it more likely that a reader will respond.

When a reader is used to getting emails on a certain list, they're more likely to open it and interact with it in some way. And if the list owner makes the introduction to your brand, they'll be even more likely to click through to perform the action you request.

If you do resort to this process, make a big offer. You had better put something in front of the person that really matters to them, because the pressure to impress is highest when you've not been given permission to email this group before.

With each level of permission comes a lower responsibility to deliver. This means that the more comfortable someone is with receiving your emails, the lower the risk of upsetting them is. While I am not promoting careless email marketing, there are times when you are more free to make mistakes or deliver "weaker" emails. A purchased list is not one of them.

If you are interested in purchasing lists – or finding out if there are lists that fit your needs – search "email lists" on Google or visit the "Getting Started" page on my blog: www.zachhellermarketing.com/email-marketing.

2. Gateways to exclusive content.

"You can see our whitepaper on the most popular way to get involved with Social Media, but first you have to give us your email address."

This is a popular way for companies to get email addresses that they can then use in future marketing. It's one of the main reasons that people create exclusive content in the first place.

Using an email request as a key to something else ensures that the person is freely giving you their email address. In this day and age, most people realize that anything they type into any website is being watched and/or collected. So most people who enter their email address know to expect a future email.

However, it's still a risky practice to use these email addresses to start sending out special offers. They've given their email address so that they can see something, or have something, and most likely that's all they want. If you start sending them offers for different products, or you flood their inbox with junk, they will likely unsubscribe or complain as quickly as they had signed up.

The best way to use lists you collect in this fashion is to continue to give them exclusive content. Send them information on events or reports that relate to the thing they already expressed interest in. Include in those emails a marketing message, but make it more subtle, and mixed in with valuable information.

3. Be a straight shooter.

When appropriate, tell the consumer exactly what they can expect when they give you their email address:

"Enter your email address to be included on our weekly Newsletter", or "Submit your email address to receive any future deals and promotions from The Company, Inc."

Doing this ensures that you capture email addresses of highly interested people. This will make each email that you send out perform that much better. It will give you confidence in your list, and in the quality of names that you have.

The downside is that a list created in this fashion will tend to grow more slowly, and if you don't have something that people want, you'll have a hard time getting them to sign up. It's more likely that this will work with Newsletters than other kinds of marketing email.

There are other, more obscure ways to collect emails. Most of them involve some sort of incentive, and therefore are most similar #2 on the previous page, "Gateways to exclusive content." But no matter how you get the email address, the second thing you have to worry about is whether or not it's a valid email.

If I can enter any combination of characters into a box and hit enter, and be taken directly to whatever it is I wanted to see, and then odds are that I'm not going to give you my actual email address. As a consumer, my email inbox is sacred. To get in there, you have to be special. And if you're not smart enough to get in there on your own, I'm not going to go out of my way to help you.

Most consumers feel the same way. They're cautious about the information that they give.

To protect against getting fake email addresses, you can use some tools that are available to you. You can use programming to validate that there is an @ sign and a period (.) with letters after it. That will at least ensure that it's formatted as an email address, which is a good first step.

The best way to get people to give you valid email addresses is to force them to receive an email before advancing. You can use tools that are available to you online or get a programmer to put this in place pretty simply. Send an email immediately after collecting their information and make them click on a link to continue or to view the exclusive content.

Not only does this make it more likely that your marketing efforts to that person will be more effective, but it also protects your sender. If you attempt to send too many emails to invalid, or fake, addresses, the service that you are using to send the emails will think you are a spammer. (We'll go over this in more detail in Section Five).

It's important to understand what people expect from you. Someone's expectations will affect how they interact with the email that you send them:

- When you purchase a list, you have no previous interaction, and it makes it hard to get opens and clicks (the two small battles you must win with every email).
- When you incentivize someone to sign up and email them something completely different, you are forcing the person to make a split second decision about how comfortable they are with you in their inbox. Most times you will lose that battle.
- When you email someone a Newsletter that they explicitly asked for, you are fulfilling a request and are not a nuisance.

Understanding why someone gives you their email address is just as important as any other strategic decision. When Groupon gets a new email address, it's likely that the person on the other end of that address is excited to receive their first email. That has to be the goal, even if you don't think that it's an achievable one for you or your company.

When people see something that they don't expect, they are more likely to ignore it. If they've signed up for a Newsletter, and they're used to getting a Newsletter, don't assume they'll be open to receiving a "10% off our products" email.

Now that you have a better idea of how and where to get the email addresses of consumers that you can market to, you need to decide when the best time to email them is. It's not as easy as just going with your gut; and we'll cover every aspect of timing in Section Four.

Section four: WHEN

When you send your emails matters. The quicker you understand this, the better results you'll get.

Sending emails as part of an overall marketing plan is a science more than an art, and timing is one of the best examples of where that science has been explored. The tests have been done, the analysis has been compiled, and the results are there for us to dissect.

A quick Google search on email marketing tests will show you a number of scattered results. But here, I've put together the most important facts (and opinions) for you to know before getting started.

1. Day of the week

"Friday is the most popular day of the week to send out promotional emails, with 42% of US Online Retailers sending at least one promotional email." - *Smith-Harmon* "Retail Email Unsubscribe Benchmark Study" (2010)

If you're like me, you are connected to email non-stop from about 9am on Monday morning to 6 p.m. on Friday. I work full time, and am constantly connected to my email account through my work computer and my mobile phone. My phone also keeps me connected to email over the weekend. But depending on the day, I may be more or less likely to respond to a marketing or promotional email that I get.

But maybe you're not like me. Or maybe the people you're marketing to are not like me. That is perfectly acceptable, and is a great reason to know as much as you can about your email lists. Not only will that change the message, it will change how and when you get it to them.

Monday is a day when most of the email-using world is returning to work after the weekend. Most times, there will be a slight buildup of emails that were not tended to over the weekend. If your promotional email happens to fall in this batch of untamed email because you send it out Monday morning, the chances of getting deleted as part of a mass delete by the end user are high.

Another reason why Monday is commonly avoided by most email marketers is because it tends to be one of the busier workdays of the week. Though it gets a bad rap for being a slow day because people have a weekend hangover, it's actually a very productive day because people are "making up for lost time." And the busier someone is, the less you can expect them to care about your email.

Tuesday, on the other hand, is the first day that people are back into the normal swing of things. Their inbox is clean, their mind is clear, and the long week of work is already underway, making it more tolerable. Many email marketers will tell you that Tuesday is the best day to send out promotional emails.

Wednesday and Thursday are also strong days in terms of marketing email performance. Like Tuesday, the work week has progressed enough so that the initial "busy" period is over. Email inboxes are kept mostly clear for the week, making it less likely that your message will be competing with others for a reader's attention.

According to the *Smith-Harmon* Retail Email Unsubscribe Benchmark Study, Friday was 2010's most popular day to send out a promotional email. There are arguments for and against sending your emails on Friday.

On the negative side, it can be argued that Friday is so close to the weekend that people have a one track mind. They are thinking about the weekend, about getting off of work, about relaxing. And an email from you won't even penetrate their consciousness. But others will tell you that Friday is the perfect day to announce a weekend sale, because most people use the weekend to do their shopping or take care of non-work related business.

I think that Friday emails are a good idea, but it depends more on the type of email than the rest of the week would. A Newsletter on a Friday will get fewer readers, and therefore you should get those our earlier in the week. An email about something that is happening over the weekend, like an event or a sale, should be sent on a Friday because it fits the mindset of your audience on that day.

Weekends are out of the question. The stats will tell you that Saturday and Sunday are the black holes of email marketing. Feel free to test it yourself, but most people do not pay close attention to their emails over the weekend, and are more likely to delete emails from people that they don't know when they check in.

2. Time of day

> "People are receptive to marketing emails during the first hour of their work day. Pure360 reports 16.5% of emails in the study were opened between 9 a.m. and 10 a.m." - *Pure360* (2009)

Most marketers understand that the day of the week that their emails go out will affect the response that they get. But they are less likely to think about the time of day that their email goes out. In reality, both are equally important and should be considered each and every time that you send out an email.

Just like any other advertisement, when people see it will affect whether or not they will be receptive. What else are they doing at the time that could distract their attention? Are they in a hurry? Are they busy? Are they paying attention?

If you see a commercial on TV right before rushing out the door to get to work you're less likely to be affected by it than someone who is relaxed and sitting on their couch. If you see a shoe ad online while doing a search for new shoes you're more likely to click on it than someone who is looking for the weather in Santa Fe.

The most important thing that you need to do is think about your audience. What does a normal day look like for them? If you're marketing to people in their 30s and 40s, they might work full time. If you're marketing to teens and 20-somethings, they might have school. Envision their day, thinking about when they are most likely to get email, when they are most likely to be busy, and when they might be ready to spend money.

The majority of Americans that you will market your products or services to will work full time. At work, it's likely that they check their email. For that reason, the large majority of marketers choose to send out promotional emails during normal business hours. You'll want to get your email in front of people at a time when you feel most of them are easily able to check email and have few distractions to keep them from reading.

In general, the earlier in the day you get to someone, the less likely that work or other things are piling up in front of them. Therefore they're more likely to have time to check email and read messages that catch their eye. But if you go too early, than you're likely to land in a crowded inbox before someone logs in to check their email that morning. If you choose to wait until late in the day, after people are home from work or school, you're taking a risk that they don't check their email until the next morning. Again, you'll be competing with a lot of other emails for opens (each person that opens your email).

Surveys by many top marketing firms have shown that the majority of Americans check email first thing when they get to work, than again during or after lunch. If I had my choice, I'd love for them to see my email during lunch as they might be more likely to whip out the credit card at that time than first thing in the morning.

The last thing to consider concerning time of day is the time difference. This one gets by most marketers when they first start. If you time your email to go out at 10am but you're on the east coast, you're hitting the west coast at 7 a.m. You can either break up your list by region (if you have the data and capability) or you can pick a time in the middle so that nobody is getting it too late, and nobody is getting it too early.

3. Holidays

Holidays have a way of really shaking things up for marketers. They can either kill you or save you. It depends what you're selling and how you're selling it. You can always run tests, but you should decide which holidays, if any, you want to target in your email campaigns long before they come.

Most marketers try to appeal their products to the holiday season. Email inboxes and physical mail boxes fill to the brim with special offers just in time for the holiday season. It's gotten to the point that this practice has gone too far, with companies trying too hard to apply the holiday of the moment to their product (when most times it's the furthest thing from relevant).

If there is no obvious way to tie your product into a holiday, than my advice is to skip it altogether. Instead, scope out a few "less familiar" holidays that many other marketers will miss out on. You can tie your product or offer into those and stand out from the crowd. Or maybe come up with your own holiday which you can celebrate however you like.

For a complete list of existing holidays, visit http://www.holidaysmart.com/

The point is, the more your emails compete with others for readers, the less likely they are to get read. And if your email is sent near a major holiday, with a special offer relating to that holiday, you are guaranteeing that your email is just another one in the batch. So either stand out from the crowd or avoid holiday email sending altogether.

4. Exceptions to the rule

As with anything else, there are exceptions to the rules stated in this section. When sending out announcements about an event or a deadline – something more time-specific – it may require you to send an email at a time or day that might not have been recommended above.

Nothing here is set in stone. I am 99% certain that there are marketers in the world who will disagree with my assertions about email marketing. So my advice to you is to not be afraid to test anything.

We've talked about what you're going to send, why you're going to send it, and when you're going to send it. But up until now, we have not discussed *where* you're going to send them from. Where do you go? How do you create and send an email? The next section will answer these questions.

SECTION FIVE: WHERE

> "20% of email in the United States and Canada is still not making it to the inbox while 3% of email goes to the "junk" or "bulk" folder and another 16% goes missing." - *Return Path* (2010)

16% of email goes missing. 16% of your email won't even get into the junk mail folder. You're already losing the battle before you even send an email.

So how do you ensure that the majority of your emails get into the inbox? Well, the first thing that you can do is go back and re-read Section One to learn how subject lines, content, from addresses, and reply-to addresses will impact the likelihood your email gets read. And second, you can use a well-known, easy-to-use email sending tool.

There are a number of companies out there that are dedicated to helping you get your emails out to the public. They have different features which you may or may not be interested in, depending on how advanced your email programs will be. They've mastered the art and science of sending marketing emails, and you should take advantage of what they have to offer.

Below are a couple of guidelines to help you in selecting which one of them to use.

1. Pricing

There are many different levels of pricing in this industry, depending on what it is that you need. Obviously, any good email marketing service is a step above sending emails out yourself. The free version of email marketing would be having a list so small that you could send the emails from your personal address without using any of the services I mention here. While this may be free, it also means that you need to get more names on your list, and it offers nothing in the way of tracking or customization, which we know is important in any email marketing campaign.

Most companies will offer a tiered pricing system, with prices depending on either the number of emails that you send out in a given time period or the number of subscribers that you have. It's important to compare more than just the price of one service versus another though, because some have more advanced features which you'll find useful once you're off and running.

Typically, you will end up paying a flat monthly fee, starting on the lower end and building up as you increase the size of your list and the frequency of your mailings. You may also be charged more if there are things that you want to do that don't come with the standard package.

To start, you should do your research. Do a search, visit websites, and make some calls. Find out what is out there, and keep a list of the benefits of each. Here are a few places to start:

- iContact.com
- ConstantContact.com
- MailChimp.com
- ExactTarget.com
- Campaigner.com

And here is a bonus tip. Don't sign up for any of them at the listed price. If you speak with someone in their sales department and have a little patience, you will most definitely be offered an initial discount. Be sure to note any discounts that you're offered so that when it does come time to sign up, you can save a little money.

2. Personalization

One of the major areas of difference between the services outlined above and the others that you will find in your search is the ability to use personalization in the emails. Personalization is an important part of email marketing, because the more you can make the message relevant to each individual reader, the more likely it is that you'll get a response.

When you upload a contact or group of contacts on your list to the email client of your choice, you should be able to upload more than just an email address. Depending on both the type of email that you are sending out, and the amount of information that you have collected from people when they signed up, you should be able to upload any number of things. These contact details might include first name, last name, date of birth, area of interest, gender, date of interest, etc., which could be used to not only give you more information about your subscribers, but also to provide a more personal email to each individual person on that list.

We see examples of personalization in almost every promotion email that we receive. Companies use "Dear Zach," instead of "Good morning." Some companies even use your first name in the subject line, which is usually a sign of spam. Other companies use more detailed information to make the email even more appropriate to the reader. I've received emails relating to my birthday, and others around topics that I was interested in because I had checked an additional box on a form. I've also received emails that told me when I last made a purchase, and what that purchase was.

All of these companies are using data that they have collected about me, and turning that data into content that they think I'll find interesting. That kind of personalization comes across when reading an email, because it reads more like something written specifically for you, instead of a piece of mass marketing. The internet, and email specifically, has allowed us to segment and personalize the user experience. And it's important to learn as much as you can about an email client's ability to store and use personal data to customize emails.

3. Connection to Databases

Want to put a signup form on your site and have that feed directly into your list online? Of course you do. When things work seamlessly, without the need for manual work, we're happy.

Different email clients will allow you different levels of customization to build programs like this. Without getting too technical, most providers will allow you to tap into their API (application programming interface) to connect your own programs or databases to theirs. Be sure to ask about this capability, but you may need to find a programmer in your company or in your network to work out the technical aspects for you.

When speaking to a member of their sales team, tell them exactly what you have in mind. For example, "I'd like to add a form on my site to collect someone's name, email, and birth date, and I'd like that to feed directly into a list in my account with you. Is that possible?"

Depending on their answer, you'll know how customizable their service is for you. And some companies will even offer technical assistance with setting this up, which is always a bonus.

4. Shared IP vs. Dedicated IP

Now that we've gotten into slightly more complicated topics, there will never be a better time to bring up the notion of Dedicated versus Shared IP addresses.

For most people, this will never matter. But it's still good to have a basic understanding of what is out there.

Emails are sent from IP Addresses. These IP Addresses need to be managed very closely, along with the nature of your email campaigns, to ensure successful delivery of emails. Because of anti-spam laws, and the difficulty that various email service providers like Google, Yahoo, and Hotmail have with spamming, it takes a lot of effort to be able to send high quantities of email from one place without getting trapped in the junk folder, or worse, lost completely.

It was for this reason, as well as ease of use and creative ability, that companies like iContact, Constant Contact, and the others mentioned above were created. What these companies do is own and manage thousands of IP addresses, which they monitor all the time to ensure the best deliverability for all of their clients, including you.

It's your job to avoid common spam traps and follow the rules, but it's also their job to ensure that you do your job. Since the company owns so many IP addresses, they're able to spread out all of the emails that get sent from their service. In this way, they avoid high volume on one IP address, which is a red flag in the eyes of the spam police.

This is what is known as a Shared IP solution. There is also a Dedicated IP solution, which is far more expensive and complex, but also offers the ability to do some incredible things with your email marketing programs. You will have more control over the look and feel of each individual email, the ability to design complex programs that send emails out to people over time, and control the message to each person based on more detailed criteria. This solution is designed more for larger companies with big marketing budgets.

If you're interested in finding out if a Dedicated IP solution is right for you, do some research and speak with people who have experience before committing.

Mastering the art of email marketing is difficult. But working with an email delivery service, like the ones mentioned in this Section is one of the best ways to improve your competency right away. As a client, you'll have access to a variety of services that they provide, including technical support and a wide array of educational resources.

They're the experts in sending emails that get into the inbox, get opened, and get read. Why? Because they have to be.

Now that we've discussed where to go to get the help you need for your email marketing program, we're getting close to the end of the line. The next big thing to think about is who is actually going to be reading the emails that you send. Section Six requires you to take a closer look at the people on your list in order to establish the best way to communicate with them.

SECTION SIX: WHO

"Consumers who subscribed to email Newsletters generated 34.25% more product sales." - *ConAgra Foods* case study in association with *MarketingSherpa* (2007)

A 34.25% increase in product sales is a good thing. Getting that kind of increase from a Newsletter is incredible, and it's happening all over the world. Email marketing is dominating the online marketing game, because when you give the customer what they want, in a format that they're already accustomed to, you're making it easier for them to take action.

In the first five sections of this book, we've discussed a variety of ways that you can ensure maximum efficiency and effectiveness of your email campaigns. But success in the world of email marketing comes down to the same basic principle as success in any other area of marketing, knowing your audience.

There are a lot of ways in which marketers try to get a greater understanding of their audience. Facts help. If you already have an existing business, try going to any records that you have. Any information on age, gender, areas of interest, income, or geographic data could be helpful in crafting marketing messages. If you don't have this information, a good old fashioned survey might be your next step.

The more you can learn about your current customers, the more you'll know about the kinds of people you're looking to attract. Surveys can be an important part of an email marketing campaign. If you have a list of subscribers already, consider sending them a survey to collect more information. Tell them you are looking to learn more about them so that you can better serve them. Most people will be happy to participate if the survey is brief enough. Keep it to 5-10 minutes at the most.

If you're asking yourself why this matters, think about the logistics of writing to different groups of people. If you're writing a letter to the CEO of a Fortune 500 company who you've never met, you'll probably write differently than if you were writing to an old friend. If you were writing a children's book, the language would be a lot different than a short story you were submitting to *The New Yorker*.

When you write to your audience, you're designing a message – which includes everything from your subject, to your copy, to your layout, to your color and font choices – that is catered to a specific group of people. You could write a long, thoughtful explanation of why your product is better than any of the competition, but it won't do anything for you if I can't understand it. And if the only thing your customer cares about is the price, than you just did a whole lot of writing for nothing.

What follows is a list of questions you should answer for yourself, as it will begin to give you a better understanding of who your subscribers are. If you can't answer them, don't guess. Do what it takes to find out. Depending on your company or the purpose of your list, the answers might be more vague. But it's good to get a working definition, even if you have to leave out a portion of your list that does not fit. That's called segmenting, and it's something we'll talk more about in Section Seven.

- What is the age group of your audience?

The age group of your audience is worth knowing because it will affect their comprehension of more complex messaging, their likelihood to read a longer email, and their response to various media, like images and videos. There is a fine line in the world of technology between people who have grown up with it, people who use it in their everyday lives (the digital natives), and those who are still lost on the simplest of things, like checking email.

The younger your audience is, the more comfortable they are with new technology. This is the social media crowd; used to sharing, liking, and following. They are more comfortable with video than text.

The older your audience gets, the more likely they are to know what they're looking for. They signed up with you for a reason and you had better deliver on that or they'll unsubscribe. They're also much more likely to read a longer email. And depending on where they're at in their careers, more likely to pay attention to special offers and discounts.

- What education level is your audience?

Building off of the first question, this is intended to question the language and graphical accompaniment that you intend to use in your emails. Just because one group is younger does not mean that they are less educated, so it's important to answer both separately.

It may seem obvious, but the lower the average education level of your subscribers, the simpler you'll need to make the copy and the call to action. If someone is confused at any point when looking at or reading your email, the likelihood of them continuing along to click on a link or make a purchase is next to none.

At the same time, if the content of your emails is overly simple to the point that it sounds like you're talking down to a more educated group of people, you may end up losing those subscribers. Find a good balance in the complexity of your message and its brevity.

And remember, the average reading level of things that get shared most often on the internet is very low (Grade 4-6), so if you're not sure who to write for, err on the side of simplicity.

- How wealthy is your audience?

This can be one of the trickier questions to answer directly, but can be very important. The general class, or financial position, of your subscribers will affect their response to specials and discount offers. It can also have a direct impact on the products or services that they might be interested in.

I've mentioned Groupon earlier in this book, but there are also companies out there that call themselves "the Groupon of the luxury market." When they say that, they mean that their products are more expensive, and their messaging is held to a higher standard.

You could take a $1000 product and offer it to me for 50% off, but if I spend my entire income on rent and food, how likely am I to drop $500 on your product? Know what your subscribers can afford and what their needs are financially in order to keep the messaging relevant.

- Does your audience work?

This is actually a few questions in one. Are they employed versus unemployed? Do they work versus go to school? And what do they do at work or school while they are there?

Each of those questions individually will tell you something about how to send your emails. If the answer is that your subscribers are all working age, and most of them are employed in office jobs, that will tell you something about how they receive their email that is very different than it would be if they were primarily students or construction workers.

- How does your audience read email?

According to a 2011 study by Knotice, a digital marketing services company, 20% of email sent by retailers is opened on a mobile device. Mobile devices have changed the game for marketers, and email marketers specifically need to take notice.

Knowing whether or not your readers open email on a mobile device can be difficult, but will most certainly change the way you use email to market to them. Simple and free analytics software (such as Google Analytics) can tell you what percentage of your website visitors are using mobile browsers. This will help you quantify the amount of visitors you have that have internet-ready mobile devices. The higher this number, the more likely your subscribers are to have email on their phones.

A promotional email read on a phone needs to be shorter, more direct, have a stronger subject line, and a very simple call to action. Of course, it's not possible to send a different version of your email only to be read on phones at the moment (don't count that out as a new feature that the email marketing companies release in the future), so it's important, once again, to find a middle-ground message that can work for both desktop and laptop viewing as well as mobile devices.

The topic of mobile email marketing adds a whole new level of complexity to email marketing that we will get into at another time. But the more you know about the email habits of your subscribers, the better off you will be.

We've made it through six sections, and hopefully at this point you're far more capable of putting together a successful email marketing campaign than you were when we started. Now, in addition to knowing what to send, when to send, and how to send, you know to think about who you're sending to. You should have a greater understanding of the strategy behind email marketing than most people who do this for a living. In the seventh and final section of this book, I will introduce a concept that marketers in the digital age have come to understand: Always be testing.

SECTION SEVEN: TRY THINGS, TRACK THINGS

"In 2010, 30% of total email time was devoted to commercial emails, compared to 17% in 2005." - *Merkle* "View From the Digital Inbox 2011" (2011)

Email marketing is both an art and a science. There are facts and stats and tests that you can use to make sure that your campaigns are as good as they can possibly be. There are dos and don'ts, mistakes to avoid, and case studies to learn from. But here is the thing that every marketer will tell you whether they work directly with email or not: it can always get better.

You've learned all that you can learn from this book. You know what to send, when to send it, and how to send it. You know who you're sending to, why you're sending it, and why they signed up to receive it. But no matter how much you learn, and how much you achieve with your email marketing campaigns, there is no end in sight.

The internet has changed the marketing game forever. Everything is testable. Everything is trackable. This is why I came up with the following mantra for myself: Try Things, Track Things.

Email marketing makes it easy to continue to expand on your current campaigns to improve success. Even if you think that you are doing everything right, you have to avoid falling into the trap of letting your work get stagnant. The percentage of people who open your email can always get better. The percentage of those people who then click through on one of your links can get better.

Using any one of the email marketing companies that were mentioned in Section Five, or most any others that exist, you can view statistics from each and every one of the emails that you send. You can test a new subject line to see if it gets people's attention, leads to more opens, and generates more sales. You can physically compare one to the other and say to yourself, this one is better.

Some services will allow you to conduct a split test. A split test will allow you to send only a small percentage of your list a test to determine what email works best before sending the winner to the rest of the group. Most large companies take advantage of this feature, and if you have the ability, I recommend giving it a try. You may learn something that you never expected to learn.

For example, you can split test something as simple as the subject line to see if one creates more opens than the other. Or you can send one version of an email with lots of graphics and imagery, and another bare bones version, that offers the text and nothing else, to see which one gets more clicks. This is a safe and efficient way to test things because you're choosing a winner before the majority of your list even gets the email.

Here are some other things worth trying:

- Test using the person's name in the subject line to see if this creates more opens.
- Test dollar amounts versus percentage discounts when offering a deal to see which creates more sales.
- Test an email with a signature versus one without.
- Test text links versus buttons and images.
- Test different headlines within your actual email.
- Test including a testimonial from a satisfied customer.

I know that a lot of people out there will say that email marketing is just one function of their job, and it's easier to get things right and continue to do them one way so that you have more time for other things. I think there is value in getting things right and replicating processes. This saves time. And time is money. But the internet has a funny way of making us feel completely comfortable with where we're at right before the game changes completely. So even if you don't test something new every time you send out an email, it's important to track your performance to see if those strong statistics start slipping.

The most important thing to remember is that the work is never done. Email, as part of a larger marketing strategy, is a way for marketers in today's world to reach people quickly and efficiently. You should continue to work on your campaigns to generate larger lists, more opens, and greater sales. You should find that using some of the tips and tricks provided in this book will start to improve the relative success of any existing campaigns that you might have.

If you're looking for inspiration, check out http://emailium.com/, a free (for now) filterable search engine of thousands of email campaigns.

For a complete Email Marketing Starter Kit, you can visit www.zachhellermarketing.com/email-marketing. There, I have provided a list of resources and add-ons to this book, which will help you start to take advantage of the tips I've provided.

Happy Sending!

www.ingramcontent.com/pod-product-compliance
Lightning Source LLC
Chambersburg PA
CBHW080605060326
40689CB00021B/4942